15-MINUTE MEDITATION

for health & wellbeing

Sam May

Copyright 2017 Sam May

Print Edition

ISBN: 9781520872308

Table of Contents

Chapter 1:
Introduction

Meditation has been practised for thousands of years in a variety of cultural and religious settings around the world. All the great world religions include some form of meditation, as a means of pursuing one's spiritual goals. However meditation is not exclusive to religious use. In recent decades, with the dawn of modern technology, there has been a growing interest in the scientific workings of meditation as a method for promoting health and wellbeing.

There is increasing evidence to support the health benefits of meditation. Studies have shown an association between regular meditation and a reduced need for health care. Meditation has been found to help in the alleviation of chronic pain which is not otherwise responding to standard medical treatment, as well as in reducing high blood pressure, muscular tension, stress, anxiety, depression, and insomnia.

Meditation is not just about sitting quietly, but is something that can pervade our whole life. To appreciate this fully we need to understand how to make meditation count in our daily experience, so that we can be more centred, present, alive and engaged in everything that we do. In meditation we learn to be fully aware of something, such as our breath, and developing this awareness helps us to become more awake in each present moment. This involves a lot of letting go, clearing the inner 'clouds' that obscure our awareness and the clarity of our perception.

The ability to let go requires contentment, being content with, in this case, the experience of our breath. There's no reason why we can't be content with something as simple as our breath, but these days we feel a need to have the TV or computer on, or to be talking or texting on our mobile phones, or to have some other form of external stimulation. There's such a drive in our culture for external stimulation, and a growing internal need for it, arising from our collective discontent. Developing the internal quality of contentment is one of the key benefits of meditation.

Another quality that we develop in meditation is acceptance. Accepting ourselves is the key here, because when it comes to meditation there's a part of our mind that likes to judge – our self, our progress, and our meditation practice. In fact there's almost constant judgement taking place in our mind, judgement of our thoughts, feelings, other people and so on. On the one hand, meditation involves subduing our neediness and discontent, and on the other hand, it involves silencing our internal critic and finding a place of acceptance in our minds.

A third quality that we develop in meditation is that of being fully present. The feeling of being more present can lift us out of negative mental states, and make us feel more positive. A lot of the happiness and excitement that we experience in our life is unstable, like a house of cards that easily collapses. It is dependent on changeable and unreliable factors of which we have little or no control. However the conscious awareness that we develop in meditation gives rise to a vibrant experience of life that is rooted in direct perception.

Through practising the fifteen-minute meditation explained in this book, you will naturally develop and come to appreciate these qualities of contentment, acceptance and awareness within your own experience.

Chapter 2:
Meditation and Health

Meditation is a process of actively calming the mind. I use the word 'actively' because sometimes our mind naturally becomes calmer than it is when we're in a certain setting, such as listening to some peaceful music, having a massage, or staring at a candle for example, but these things in themselves are not meditation. The meditation that I'm talking about is the active process of calming our mind, which involves conscious effort. For example staring at a candle is really just a visual exercise, in which we are focusing our eyes. What we're doing with our mind when we're staring at a candle is anybody's guess! We might be thinking about our shopping list or what we're having for dinner. In itself this is not meditation because it doesn't involve a conscious effort to calm our mind.

What we're going to be learning in this book is how to train our mind to become more still and calm. In this sense we're going to be doing some mental exercise, a mental 'workout'. This is very much like going to the gym. When we go the gym, we exercise our biceps and triceps and various other muscles. In meditation we're going to be exercising our mindfulness and concentration and other mental 'muscles' to develop calm and stillness inside.

Meditation is not necessarily a religious exercise. It depends what we're focusing on. If you follow a particular religion, then I hope that the explanations in this book will fit in with and perhaps even enhance your religious practices. If you don't follow any particular religion but are perhaps interested in the general notion of spirituality, then certainly this book can help you to cultivate your spirit. But even if you're not interested in spirituality or religion and you just want to be more healthy and have an improved sense of well-being, primarily this book will help you to achieve that, as the title suggests.

In this context the ultimate goal of meditation is to achieve our optimum health on an internal level, which I believe will extend to a physical level as well. For example, let's think about the tension in our body and how that relates to our mind. This is a good example of how the body and mind work together and interrelate. To provoke some contemplation, I'm going to propose that all of our physical tension is a manifestation of tension in our mind. When we first do the relaxation meditation that I'm going to explain shortly, we're probably going to discover areas of tension in our body that we didn't even know existed. There is so much tension throughout our body, some on a very gross level and some on a more subtle level. Sometimes we're painfully aware of it. Where is this tension in our body coming from? Why do certain parts of our body tense up? Generally speaking, it relates to tension in our mind - some holding on, tightness, or discomfort in our mental state.

Consider the word 'disease'. Hyphenated it looks like this: 'dis-ease'. We can observe that there is a lack of 'ease' in our mind a lot of the time. What effect does this have on our body? It makes our body tighten up. We often say to someone, 'You're uptight'. We know that when we're uptight, it's really our mind that's uptight. Our mind is wound up and waiting to snap, and our body tenses up too. This is a good example of how our mind creates discomfort in our body, which can lead on to the development of disease and sickness.

In winter-time, many people get the flu, but not everyone does. Why do some people get the flu and not others? A doctor would probably explain this in terms of our immune system. It's generally understood these days that our immune system is impaired when we are run down, exhausted, stressed, or overdoing it in some way. When we're having a hard time emotionally there's a basis there for our immune system to break down. When that happens we're more prone to invasion from the common cold and flu. In this way we can understand that even things like the flu virus has an internal causative factor. Without that internal disharmony, we can to some extent protect ourselves from this kind of illness. This is an example of how our mind plays a part in the development of illness.

It would be quite bold to say that all sickness and disease stems from the mind. However from the point of view of my own experience I generally believe this to be true. Obviously there are some more serious illnesses which we have to think about more carefully, and some people are born with certain illnesses. These raise bigger questions which require a more thorough investigation if we are to propose that all disease begins in the mind. Such a detailed investigation is beyond the scope of this book. However I would say that it's something to think about. As an acupuncturist, I often see people with quite serious health conditions where there's clearly an element of emotional distress that appears to have triggered or stimulated the origins of that illness. Perhaps a big life event, such as a divorce or the loss of a loved one for example, has precipitated a chain reaction of ill health which ultimately manifests as something quite serious. We can probably testify to this at some level in our own experience or in the experiences of people that we know. It's certainly challenging to think that there might be an emotional cause of our illnesses and certainly for anyone with a more serious illness it can be very challenging at times to face that possibility. Nevertheless it can be very healing if we can see that there is an emotional element involved. It can enable us to go back to the actual roots of the problem and heal ourselves on a deeper level. Meditation can help us in this process, by promoting a more profound awareness of the situations we experience in our lives. As I said earlier, it can help us to become more content, more accepting, more aware, and more healthy from the inside.

This is a basic overview of how meditation can help us to improve our health and well-being. In the immediate sense meditation can help us to relax on both a mental and physical level, but it can also help in the recovery and prevention of illness, and in the longer term it imbues us with certain positive internal qualities that can be of immense value in our lives - the qualities of contentment, acceptance, and the feeling of living our life more fully, being more aware, more awake and enjoying our experience more every day.

Chapter 3:
Relaxation Meditation

In this chapter I'm going to explain a relaxation meditation. Essentially this involves scanning through our body from head to toe and relaxing all the muscles. We gently focus on each area, identifying any tension or tightness there and then just gently allow that area to relax. We can imagine the tension melting or dissolving away. Hopefully you'll find at the end of this exercise that your body will be in a deeply relaxed state, and as a result your mind will also feel more relaxed. Our mind starts to relax as our body relaxes. In our daily life it's as if our mind uses our body to hold onto things, and this creates tension in our body. Our body is like the instrument of our mind. When our mind has stopped expressing itself in our body and gathers inwards, it feels much more relaxed. On one level we could think of our body as a manifestation of the mind. Generally speaking, every movement that our body makes originates in our mind, either in our conscious mind or our unconscious mind. In this sense our bodies can be thought of as just a physical level of our minds. If we think in this way our mind definitely becomes more relaxed.

If we're a beginner or if we've not done any meditation for a long time, we may find ourselves getting sleepy in the meditation. If we do fall asleep, don't worry - it's not the end of the world! Don't beat yourself up about it. In a way, if we fall asleep in meditation, it's better than not doing any meditation at all. At least we will have had a restful experience. Generally I would say that if we do happen to fall asleep in the process of trying to meditate, it's more restful than just falling asleep in front of the TV for example. The problem here is that our mind is not really used to slowing down or switching off other than in the context of going to sleep, and therefore meditation is a new experience for our mind. It's a bit like going to sleep but it's not actually going to sleep. It involves going into a deeper state of mind, but without actually falling to sleep - we're going to stay awake. It takes some time to become clear in our own experience about the distinction between sleep and the meditative state. Gradually though we get more used to this and then it becomes easier for us. But in the beginning, if you fall asleep occasionally, don't worry. It's 'par for the course'!

In terms of posture, the most important thing is having a straight back, which helps to keep us awake, and for this purpose upright chairs are ideal. Some people prefer to sit on the floor, in the more traditional cross-legged posture for example, especially if they are familiar with yoga and other postural disciplines. This traditional posture has some spiritual significance and may give some subtle advantage at a more advanced level of practice, but for beginners at least it is quite adequate to sit in an upright chair.

It's important to be comfortable. If we sit in a reclining chair, we're probably going to have more trouble staying awake. If we're sitting in a chair, it's best to have our feet flat on the floor without crossing over our legs. Our hands can just rest in our lap, placed on top of each other, centred. Alternatively we can place our palms on our thighs. Our eyes should be gently closed, but not tightly closed - enough to block out any visual distraction, but allowing a little bit of light in, like a door left ajar. This is especially helpful if we're sleepy. The eyes should be closed in a relaxed way, without tensing at all. Ideally we should breathe through our nostrils, unless we've got a blocked nose in which case we'll have to breathe through our mouth. The nose is preferable as the mouth can easily dry up or start drooling (which can be embarrassing in a group setting!).

Relaxation meditation:

Begin the meditation by scanning through your body, starting at the top of your head, from the crown of your head right along to your forehead. Try to identify any areas of tension or tightness. Then right down your forehead to your eyebrows. Gently focus on these areas and allow the skin and muscles to relax completely. Right around your eyes and eyelids. Imagine the tension melting away, dissolving away. Right down your face, and through your cheeks and jaw, letting go of any clenching or tightness. Right across to the back of your neck and into your shoulders. Allow your shoulders to drop. Scan through your neck and shoulders, identifying any tension or tightness there. Imagine the tension melting away. Then all the way down your shoulders, scanning through to the tops of your arms, and down to your elbows, right down your forearms, through your wrists and hands, all the way to the tips of your fingers, identifying any tension and gently letting go, allowing the muscles to relax. And you can scan back up your arms again into your shoulders and then down your back, right around your shoulder blades, through your chest and heart centre, identifying any tightness or discomfort and letting go. Right through your stomach and abdomen, identifying all discomfort there. Allow everything to relax.

Right through into your lower back. Imagine the tension flowing away. Through to your pelvis and buttocks and into the tops of your legs, down your thighs. Any tension you find, allow the muscles to relax. Scan through your knees, down your calves, letting go of any tightness there. Right down to your feet, through your ankles, heels, and down to the tips of your toes, imagining all the tension dissolving away.

Having relaxed your whole body in this way, spend a moment observing and enjoying this experience, feeling a greater sense of lightness in your body. And, then gently in your own time, relax your concentration and rise from the meditation.

Doing this relaxation meditation helps us to become aware of where we personally hold tension in our body. In this respect everyone is different. For example, some people hold all their tension between their eyebrows, some hold it all in their shoulders and some hold it all in their stomach. It really varies from person to person so it's important that we personally get a sense of how we hold our tension.

As a practical exercise we can look and see in our daily activities where we tense up and where our body holds tension. Then just gently focus on those areas and let the tension go. Whatever we're doing, as soon as we become aware of the tension, just let it go. Through this practice alone, we start to relax more because for the most part we are generally unaware of the tension we hold in our body. We go day after day without really paying any attention to it until something snaps or something goes wrong. If we can actually be aware of it as it starts developing, we can then easily 'nip it in the bud' and put it back to normal. This meditation can give us a sense of how our body can feel when it's really relaxed, and there's no reason why we can't maintain that. Being aware and noticing the tension is half the battle.

It's also possible that this meditation can make us feel more grounded in our body. Sometimes we can feel disconnected from our bodies. This exercise definitely gives us a greater awareness of our own body. Often people experience a weightless feeling when doing this meditation, as though parts of their body, such as their hands, feel like they are disappearing. The tension we normally experience is quite a substantial sensation, so when that's gone there can be a feeling of lightness. Certainly, feeling more present in our body is a good outcome, inducing a more grounded feeling.

At this stage we're not specifically stilling our mind. We're just getting our body relaxed first, preparing ourselves for the main meditation to follow. The reason for doing this each time at the beginning of our meditation sessions is to give us a head start in terms of actually stilling our mind. As I explained earlier, the body is like a manifestation of the mind. When we release our tension on a physical level, there's less work for us to do on our mind. Jumping straight in to the practice of settling our mind is more challenging, because we are unlikely to have properly resolved the physical manifestations of our internal tension. These need to be dealt with first before we can really still our mind. This is why we start with this relaxation exercise, gathering our mind into our body and resolving our physical tension.

In order to do this relaxation meditation, we need to turn our mind to each area of the body and become aware of what's going on there. We may initially find no tension at all in certain areas, but if we look more closely we may discover some subtle tension or tightness there. As soon as we become aware of any tension, it immediately starts to resolve. In relation to this practice we need to think of our mind as 'awareness'. For example, when we turn our attention to the sensations in our knees, we simply become aware of the sensations in our knees. We don't need to conceptualise or think analytically about the sensations. We just simply become aware.

The process of meditation is different from the conceptual processes that we engage in all day long. This relaxation meditation, for example, has a non-conceptual element to it, in the sense that we don't have to verbalise anything in the meditation. It's a question of moving our awareness through our body, gradually taking our focus and attention from head to toe and observing the various sensations. There are forms of meditation which actually involve internal verbalisation, such as meditating on a mantra or meditating on a positive emotional state, such as compassion. In the case of compassion for example, we express our feelings internally with words in order to maintain that state of mind. Without this process of internal verbalisation, it's very difficult to hold onto a state of mind like this. However the kind of meditation that we're doing here doesn't involve internal verbalisation. We can think of it as a non-conceptual awareness, in that it doesn't involve 'thinking' in the usual sense of the word. It's like 'thinking without sound'.

The focus required in meditation is a gentle one. The concept of concentration that most of us have is of a furrowed brow, involving an element of tension, as in the famous image of

'The Thinker' for example. From the point of view of meditation, this isn't really concentration. It involves pushing and trying too hard. The effort that we need to apply in meditation involves simply placing our mind on something. There's a gentleness in this process, free from tension. For example, when we put a cup on a table, we just place it on the table. We don't have to force it onto the table. Meditative concentration is like this. It's about 'placing' our mind.

Chapter 4:
Mindful Breathing Meditation

In this chapter I'm going to explain how to do the breathing meditation which is on the accompanying audio MP3. I'm going to give a broad overview of the breathing meditation now, and then in the following chapters I'm going to explore some of the more intricate elements of and skills involved in the practice of meditation. The primary objective of this chapter is to give you a good understanding of how to do the meditation, so that you can start to do it on your own, with or without the MP3. Ultimately you can do the meditation without the MP3, and some people prefer to do it like this from the start, but generally it's a useful aide to help you get started. If you do it on your own without the MP3, you essentially have to guide yourself through the meditation. This is why it's helpful to do the meditation with guidance at the beginning so that you then know how to guide yourself through it later on. At that point you would effectively be able to guide someone else in the meditation as well. It's eventually a case of becoming your own meditation 'guide', which comes from familiarity with the process and flow of the meditation as well as gradually building your confidence. You could start doing it on your own from the very beginning, but it might be more helpful to start with a combination, for example using the MP3 regularly, but also fitting in some extra sessions without it, even just for five minutes here and there.

Although this is a breathing meditation, in one sense it's not really about the breath. The breath, in this case, happens to be the 'object' of meditation, in that it's the thing that we're focusing on. However the real training in this practice is developing our mindfulness. There are other kinds of breathing meditation that you may have heard about or encountered, such as counting the breath or perhaps controlling our breath in some way, breathing very deeply for example. There is a popular meditation in which we breathe in for a certain number of seconds and then breathe out for a certain number of seconds and so on. This is an example of controlled breathing. In this meditation, we're not going to control our breathing at all.

The focus or object of the meditation, what we're actually going to be concentrating on, is the subtle sensation of the breath at the tip of our nostrils, as it passes in and out. This sensation is really quite subtle. It's not something that most of us have ever really thought about or tuned in to, so it might take some time just to get used to it, to identify it in our own experience and to know what it feels like. It's helpful to spend a few minutes trying to get a clear sense of what it is that we're supposed to be focusing on here.

In this meditation we're going to allow ourselves to breathe naturally. We're not going to modify our breathing at all. In general there are many ways that we can improve the way that we breathe, but for the purposes of this meditation we're not going to be focusing on these aspects of breathing. As mentioned above, this practice is really about developing our mindfulness. Certainly this meditation has the effect of harmonising the mind and the breath, which softens our breathing and makes it more relaxed, more comfortable and more gentle - but this is not the goal of this meditation. It is ultimately a mental exercise. What we're doing is training and controlling our mind through developing our mindfulness.

In this meditation we focus our attention on the sensation of the breath at the tip of our nostrils, the subtle sensation that we feel there as the breath enters and exits. Remember to allow the breath to flow naturally, without manipulating it or controlling it in any way. We simply use the breath as the focal point for our mind. People often ask whether meditation involves 'emptying the mind'. If we try to empty our mind, we will find that we can't actually empty it completely because the mind is always aware of something. In meditation we give our mind one thing to focus on, something calming and settling. There is always a focal point in meditation, as explained previously.

The first step then is identifying our focal point, which is what we call the 'object' of meditation. We can spend a few minutes doing this initially, to become familiar with whatever it is that we've chosen to focus on. Once we've established our focus, we then need to understand what to do with our mind in the meditation. Ideally we need to concentrate our attention single-pointedly on the sensation of our breath. We are aiming to concentrate our mind in a meditative way which involves placing or resting our attention on the mind in a relaxed way, without forcing or pushing it in any way, just holding it there gently. There's an element of balance involved here, which I'll discuss in more detail later.

During the meditation our mind is going to want to go elsewhere, away from the breath, and there will be all sorts of thoughts and distractions coming up. We have to keep bringing our attention back to the breath, again and again. This is training in mindfulness, and to begin with this process of bringing our mind back to the breath again and again is the main thing we need to be doing. I'll be discussing the development of mindfulness in more detail later on. In the space of a fifteen-minute session we might bring our attention back to the breath over 100 times, which might sound alarming, but actually that's the way it is at the beginning for most of us. Our minds are very unruly, and it's very difficult for us to keep our attention held on the breath for more than a few seconds without another thought taking our attention away. So as soon as we notice that our mind has wandered away from the breath, we just need to bring it back.

There's skill involved in doing this effectively. We need to learn to retrieve our attention without any internal commentary or judgement. For example we might start thinking about how we're doing or how distracted we are. Once we start going down the road of internal commentary and judgement, we start spinning another wheel of distraction in our mind, which just creates further disturbance. When we find that we're distracted, we just need to bring our mind straight back to the breath. There's no need to comment or judge. Doing this effectively involves accepting our level of ability, whatever level we're at. For as long as we're trying our best, we're doing perfectly. Actually that's all we can do. We should try not to compare ourselves to anyone else, or to how we think we should be doing, because we are simply at the level that we're at. We have to accept that and just try our best. If we try our best, we've done well.

Sometimes we might not notice that we're distracted for a while, perhaps even for several minutes. If this happens, don't make a big drama out of it, just bring the attention back to the breath. We can only do the best we can. Don't judge or comment in any way. This is training in acceptance, which I've mentioned previously, and this state of acceptance is a beautiful internal quality to develop. In this context it means being accepting of the thoughts that are coming up in our mind, not judging them. A lot of our mental strain in meditation relates to an internal battle that stems from non-acceptance, so developing this quality makes the whole process much easier. Furthermore, the more accepting we are of ourselves, the more accepting and warmly disposed we will feel towards other people as well, so there are broader positive benefits here.

I also mentioned previously about being content with the object of our meditation. Contentment is another quality that we'll develop through meditation. In this case, we are learning to be content with our breath, just enjoying the quiet, natural rhythm of our breath. There's no need for us to think about anything else. Just enjoy the breath moment by moment, allowing our mind to rest. Although the correct meditative state is restful we are also fully awake in it. Our mind is fully alert and present, but resting as well, feeling still and settled.

Initially we might spend the whole session just bringing our mind back to the breath again and again. This is a bit like training a puppy to walk alongside us. If we've got a crazy puppy that just wants to charge around all the time, we have to keep asking it to come back or pulling it back on a lead until it starts to learn to walk next to us. Our mind is a bit like this. We need to keep bringing it back again and again until it starts to get the message and remain for longer periods with the object.

To begin with, fifteen minutes is a good length of time for a meditation session. It gives us enough time to unwind and get into a genuinely relaxed state, but it's not too long to result in a loss of quality. It's very much about quality over quantity in the beginning. If we give ourselves an hour to meditate, for example, the chances are that we're going to have quite a challenging session, most of which is going to be half-hearted. If we give ourselves fifteen minutes, we can be really focused and make a sustained effort. So it's important to get the balance right between quality and quantity. To start with it's much better to have a fully-focused fifteen minutes than it is to have a half-hearted thirty or forty minutes.

However, there's nothing magic about fifteen minutes. We can meditate for a shorter period if we want, say five or ten minutes. Five minutes may be a little short but sometimes it's useful if we want to gather our mind and we've only got a few minutes to spare. Even a five-minute meditation can be enough sometimes to centre us and restore some inner calm.

The question of how often to meditate each day is addressed in more detail later on in this book. However to start with I would recommend that, unless you've got plenty of spare time in your schedule, don't set yourself too big a goal as this can easily backfire. We can easily get discouraged if we set ourselves a schedule that we can't maintain, so it's best to start gradually. Begin by doing it once a day and see if you can maintain that. Once you've established that, then you can think about incorporating a second daily session if you wish. We need to build our meditation practice gradually - otherwise we will quickly become discouraged.

It's also important not to be too rigid about our practice. Structure is generally important, but there's a level at which we can go too far with it. Ultimately we want to get to a point where we can be dipping in and out of meditation throughout our day, throughout our life, whatever is going on around us. Whether we're walking down the street or travelling on a bus or talking with people, being able to dip in to that inner space is really valuable. The experience of meditation is ultimately something that we want to have at our fingertips. Formal meditation practice needs to be understood in conjunction with informal meditation practice. Ideally we want to be in a semi-meditative state all the time in that we want to preserve our inner space and calm continually.

Developing our mindfulness in this way is like flexing mental 'muscles'. Through this training we're building the mental muscle of mindfulness, by learning to hold our attention on the breath. By exercising in this way we're going to start to develop considerable control over our mind. The result of this is that we can resolve many of the problems in our lives, because we have the necessary internal space to choose the way we respond to difficult situations.

In general we are ruled by the circumstances that arise in our lives. If something comes up that we find difficult, the chances are that we get bowled over by it or we automatically respond in a negative way. As a result, because we don't have the ability to control our mind, we're very much at the mercy of whatever circumstances arise in our life. Due to this we experience a subtle level of fear in our mind every day - 'What's going to happen to me today?' Actually it's not about what happens to us today, it's about what we make of what happens today. The ability to choose our reality is an invaluable skill that comes from our training in meditation. We can effectively begin to choose our experience. In response to a situation that comes up in our life, we might initially start pursuing an unhappy train of thought, but through our training in meditation we have a greater ability to control and change our thought process, to the point of redirecting our mind in a more positive direction. For example, if our train is delayed, we might start to think 'This is a really annoying inconvenience,' and start to get upset about it. The truth is that we don't have to think about it in this way and get upset about it. Ultimately we have a choice. This is what most of us are missing these days, the ability to choose our response, simply because we don't have control over our minds.

Developing the ability to pull our mind back to the breath is developing the strength of mind to redirect our thoughts and ultimately to pull our mind anywhere we want. We are also developing the inner space within which to do so. This inner space allows us to recognise when our thoughts are going adrift, and also to pull our attention back and control it. This explanation offers an insight into how useful and powerful meditation training really is, in all aspects of our life. It gives us the freedom to experience our life in a more positive way.

Meditation practice involves learning new pathways of thought in our mind, enabling us to create a more positive reality. A lot of our reflexes and reactions stem from a very deep level of consciousness, but we have to start somewhere. We begin by controlling our mind at a gross level, and then gradually start to go deeper, developing our mindfulness at increasingly more subtle levels. This is discussed in more detail later in the book, but ultimately we can meditate at the very deepest levels of our consciousness. These can be accessed consciously in meditation, which is something that we can work towards over time. However a lot of our daily problems can be resolved from training our mind on a gross level.

The experience of meditation is very nourishing and people often report feeling as if they've had a good sleep. Meditation has a similar nourishing quality to sleep, but also a very relaxing effect as well, which sometimes sleep doesn't, especially if our mind is disturbed or unsettled in some way.

In fact if we have problems sleeping, meditation can help us to sleep more deeply and restfully too.

There is research to show that meditation can help with a variety of health problems, such as chronic pain for example. If we suffer from chronic pain, no amount of thinking about the pain and telling it to go away will resolve it. However if we actually take our mind completely off the pain and focus single-pointedly on the breath for example, then our pain will temporarily disappear. This is because normally part of our mind is holding on to that pain. A lot of what we call 'pain' is actually in our mind.

What is pain? There is a sensation in our body which we call 'pain', but our mind then grabs onto this and seizes up around it, and this process seems to sustain and exacerbate our pain in some way. When we take our mind off it completely, as is possible in meditation, and then come back to the sensation afterwards, it's not the same. We have a different experience. Working with pain in meditation like this is very helpful. We can learn to free ourselves from pain to some extent. Also if we actually analyse and question the sensation deeply, we can release the tight grip our mind has on it. Once we loosen this grasping on to the pain, most of the 'pain' dissolves. What's left is minimal in comparison, and not a big problem for us.

Chapter 5:

Developing Mindfulness

In this chapter I explain what mindfulness is and how we can develop it. Through understanding this clearly we can learn how to meditate correctly and also how to monitor our progress in meditation.

Some days we might feel that our meditation session was not so good, and other days we might feel that it went really well. We will start to notice that on some days our mind is more busy, and on other days our mind is more sleepy. This is what I refer to as our 'mental weather'. This mental weather is relative to our stage of development. For example, initially our mental weather might be like the weather in England, generally grey, wet, and changeable, with a lot of fluctuation. If we then move to another country, there are still weather patterns, but suppose we move to somewhere like Mauritius, the weather's going to be on an altogether different scale. However there are some fluctuations there as well. As we progress in meditation, it's not as though we achieve uniform mental weather right away. It gradually starts to become more uniform, but it's more like moving to another country with a steadier climate, where there's still some movement and fluctuation. I can't emphasise enough that for as long as we're trying, we're doing perfectly.

Mindfulness is that part or faculty of our mind that enables us to hold our attention on an object of consciousness without letting it go. In this case, the sensation of our breath at the tip of our nostrils is the object of consciousness, the thing that we're focusing on. The function of mindfulness is to keep our mind focused on our object. It's that faculty of our mind that holds our attention on something.

As we develop our mindfulness, we will become more and more capable of holding on to the sensation of our breath. Firstly we need to understand how mindfulness develops. Initially, when we start meditating, we can quite easily become overwhelmed or discouraged by the amount of busyness in our mind - the almost constant movement and incessant arising of thoughts and distractions. At the beginning there's not a huge amount that we can do about the rate at which thoughts arise in our mind. This is determined to a large extent by our 'mental weather', as I mentioned earlier. Our thoughts just keep popping up at a certain rate and there's little we can do about limiting that rate to begin with. So what do we need to aim for when we're starting out?

The first thing to concentrate on is developing our awareness of the thoughts popping up, becoming more adept at noticing our thoughts arising. In doing this we are wholeheartedly accepting the state of play in our mind, which as I've explained previously is crucial to our progress - fully accepting whatever's going on in our mind and the way our mind is behaving. We have to start from where we are.

There's an old joke that highlights this. There's an Englishman touring Ireland and he gets completely lost, so he goes up to a local Irishman and says, 'Excuse me, I'm trying to find my way to Tipperary and I'm completely lost - please could you give me some directions?'. The Irishman looks at him kindly and replies 'I wouldn't start from here if I were you!'

This joke is quite pertinent to our meditation practice because a lot of us would rather be starting from somewhere else. We don't like to accept where we're at, especially once we start to become aware of what our mental activity is really like. We don't like to face up to the apparent horror of our mind behaving like a wild animal, charging around like a bull in a china shop causing total chaos. However in order to progress in meditation we must first embrace where we're starting from, which ultimately involves accepting ourselves, accepting the way we are. It may take a while just to get to know our mind a little. Some people are quite surprised when they start meditating - 'I never realised my mind was like this and that I have so little control of it'.

In order to develop our awareness of what's going on in our mind, with part of our mind we need to step back a little from the main flow of mental activity. It's as though there's a corner of our mind that's stepping back and just watching what's going on. This is like when we're walking down a dark path at night and we're being aware of who might be behind us or what's around us. Our main attention is on the path in front of us, but there's a heightened awareness of what's going on around us. Meditation is like this, in that there's a heightened awareness that we're developing, in effect another dimension of our mind.

Accepting what's going on inside our mind gives us the space to sit back and watch, rather than getting involved in a fight with our thoughts. Wrestling with our thoughts implies non-acceptance of our internal state, not liking what we are seeing. We might start fighting against a certain thought process, criticising our thoughts, criticising ourselves, and just generally becoming quite unhappy about the whole situation. Getting involved with our thoughts in this way is the approach of a non-accepting mind, and essentially digs us into a deeper hole, disturbing our internal state even further.

Acceptance is so crucial, just learning to accept whatever's coming up. If we can cultivate this accepting approach to our thoughts , we'll find that we naturally become more accepting of ourselves as human beings as well, less self-critical, less judgmental of ourselves.

As a result of this we'll also become less critical of others. In general most, if not all, of our critical thoughts towards other people arise from feelings of inadequacy with respect to ourselves, a need to feel better about ourselves, which we achieve temporarily by thinking about how someone else looks worse. If we can accept who we are and where we're at, then we won't have any sense of feeling inadequate. We will become an accepting person in every way, not just of ourselves, but of others as well. We will feel much less critical and negative towards other people. This has further benefits for us in terms of improving our relationships with other people and generally improving the quality of our lives. All this can develop from our meditation practice, through our learning to accept what's going on in our mind.

In the beginning, learning to develop this skill is a key goal of meditation. I use the word 'goal' here, but in a way it's more like an 'anti-goal'. It's not the sort of goal that we're used to in the sense of achieving something. Instead it's like taking a step backwards, just accepting the way things are, letting go of our judgmental attitude. In this sense meditation is more about taking something off than putting something on, and it's important to keep this in mind.

So we're developing our awareness of the thoughts in our mind with an accepting attitude. When I use the word 'accepting' here I don't mean 'going along with' our thoughts. We're not getting involved with or following the thoughts that arise. We're accepting that these thoughts are arising, but we're not allowing our mind to get involved with them. What does this mean practically? Essentially it means letting go of the thoughts and bringing our attention back to the breath, again and again. It may be that we spend the whole meditation session doing just this; as soon as our attention is back to the breath, another thought sparks off, so then we bring our attention back again and another thought sparks off, and so on. It may be that just a split second after we get back to the breath another thought arises. That's ok. Just accept it. Don't get frustrated or discouraged. We just keep bringing our mind back to the breath. For as long as we're exercising this control of the mind, bringing our mind back over and over again, we'll be making good progress. This is the main thing we need to be doing at the beginning.

We needn't be concerned if we're unable to stay focused on our breath for more than a few seconds before another thought arises. As I've said previously, there's not a great deal we can do about the rate at which thoughts arise in our mind at the beginning of our practice. What we can do something about is our awareness of what's going on in our mind, and with that we can start to control our mind, letting go of distractions and bringing our attention back to the breath.

We'll probably revisit the thoughts that come up in our meditation session several times later on that day – there's generally plenty of time to pursue them afterwards if we want to. It's helpful to remember this sometimes, as it can make it easier for us to let go of them during the meditation session. We can put our thoughts on a shelf and come back to them later. Sometimes during our meditation session we might start thinking about something which turns out to be a really good idea that applies to some life situation we're dealing with for example, and we might think, 'Wow! - this is a brilliant idea I've just had and I've got to think about it right now for a few minutes'. Even in this instance we need to let go of that thought. Just put it on the shelf and come back to it later. This requires some mental strength, but we can do it. Even if we think we've solved the mysteries of the universe, just put it on the shelf and come back to it later, because from the point of view of our meditation this thought is a distraction from our focal point, and our aim here is to develop our mindfulness, which means holding our attention on one thing only.

Some people feel that meditation can be a useful environment in which to resolve personal problems and issues, and to work through difficulties. There is a way in which we can use meditation to help us work through issues that we're having, but when we're training in mindfulness meditation, the focus needs to be on developing our mindfulness. If we're doing the breathing meditation that I've explained, then we need to focus on the sensation of our breath, and nothing else. If we want to use meditation to resolve issues or reflect on things, then what I suggest is that we first do the fifteen-minute meditation exactly as I've explained, and then at the end of our fifteen-minute meditation, when we've established a calmer, clearer mental state, allow ourselves some time for reflection. It's important to do the mindfulness meditation first in its entirety before we move on to reflecting about things that are going on in our life, as opposed to mixing them together which will just interfere with the development of our mindfulness.

When we sit down to meditate, it's sometimes helpful to give ourselves permission to relax and put our daily thoughts to one side. It's hard to let go sometimes, but if we can allow ourselves to go into that place of calm, and really taste it and experience it, even if just for a few moments, then we will gradually overcome any hesitation or resistance that we may have. We will gain confidence in that state of calm.

For some people meditation can arouse fear, which is essentially a fear of the unknown, in this case going into a silent space inside. Many of us find it difficult to sit still even for one minute; the moment we sit still, we feel compelled to do something else, for example turning on the TV or the radio, or picking up a newspaper or a book, or checking our email or mobile phone. Why can't we just relax and enjoy the calm of something as simple and natural as our breathing and the quiet of our own mind? The problem is that most of us have never learnt any way of doing that, which is why meditation is so valuable. It gives us a way to find peace within ourselves without relying on any external stimulation, to find comfort within our own mind. Meditation is the method that enables us to achieve this.

Developing our mindfulness is something that will happen gradually as we apply effort. We just need to keep trying, becoming more aware and accepting, bringing our mind back again and again. At first the rate at which we start to notice our distractions will improve, in the sense that we will become more adept at noticing them taking our mind away somewhere. We'll be able to catch them more quickly. Then also the rate at which we are able to retrieve our attention and let go of those distractions will also begin to improve. There might be a delay initially, where it takes a little while to let go of the distraction after we've noticed it, but eventually we'll be able to bring our mind back more and more quickly to the breath.

These are the main ways of monitoring our development to

start with. As we improve, we will eventually reach a point where we're able to notice our mind is moving away from the breath as soon as it starts to set off, and we'll be able to bring our attention back before it's completely left the breath. This is like if we're standing on the sea-front on a very windy day holding on to the railings, and suddenly there's a big gust of wind which pulls us away, but we just manage to hold on to the railings while we're being pulled away. We're holding on still but we're being pulled in another direction. Similarly at this stage of meditation there's a feeling that we're being pulled away by a distraction, but we're just able to hold on to the breath and bring our whole attention back to it. In this way we're able to hold on to the sensation of our breath without fully letting go of it for the duration of the meditation session, at which point our mindfulness is fully developed.

Distractions still arise at this stage, but they don't pull us away completely from the breath. We might think 'I thought perfect mindfulness would mean that I'd be in perfect stillness and silence', but actually this a higher level of meditation, where distractions don't even arise in the slightest. Our mindfulness, which is the ability to hold on to the object of meditation, is developed when it's holding on to the object all the time, whether in full or in part. We're never letting go completely, but there's still some movement in the mind pulling our attention here and there, and there's still more work to do.

Settling the subtle movements of the mind is a more advanced level of meditation which we don't need to worry about too much for now. It involves finding the perfect balance in our concentration. There's a good analogy to help us understand this. When we're in the bath with a wet bar of soap, if we squeeze it too tightly it slips out of our hand, but if we don't hold it firmly enough it also slips out of our hand. There's a certain balance involved in holding the wet bar of soap, and this is the kind of balance that is ultimately required in meditation. If we push a little too much and we're holding on to our object too tightly, we create an element of tension in the mind which generates movement. A subtle form of agitation develops, and our mind starts moving around again. In this way there's a relationship between trying too hard and being distracted. Trying too hard stimulates movement in the mind, whereas if we're gently resting the mind on the object it doesn't move, just like holding that bar of soap gently such that it doesn't slip around. However if we relax a little bit too much, our concentration becomes a bit loose and starts to slip, and a hazy internal state develops where the object of meditation becomes less clear. With that comes a feeling of withdrawing and getting sleepy. This is the other extreme where we're not holding on firmly enough.

Balancing and regulating the firmness of our concentration in this way is quite subtle. However it's helpful to understand this concept from the beginning, even if it might seem beyond us at present. For most of us, to start with, it's one extreme or the other; either our mind is very busy and distracted, or we're nodding off a bit. Finding the balance between these two extremes is helpful to keep in mind when we're starting out. Initially we tend to flip from one extreme to the other; we might begin the meditation with our mind racing at a hundred miles an hour and then a few minutes into it our mind crashes out. It's like a 'crash and burn' syndrome where we're going flat out and then suddenly 'Bang', it all gets too much and our mind implodes. The middle ground, which to begin with we might only visit in passing, can take some time to get acquainted with. When our mind starts to get a bit tired or sleepy in meditation, it tends to drift off into a state of sleep because that's the only pathway it knows. It's important to find this middle ground between the two extremes of distraction and sleepiness, in our own experience, and this will come in time as our familiarity with meditation grows.

There are some other practical things that we can do to regulate our concentration in meditation. If we are sleepy and tired, we can try opening our eyes a little bit, just enough to let in a little bit of light, maybe just a millimetre; but not so much that we're visually distracted. We simply allow a little light to come in to awaken our mental state. We can also try lifting our chin up slightly if we're tired, so that our neck is straight rather than the normal position of being slightly tilted forward, and we can try straightening our back more. We can also consider taking off a layer of clothing, or opening a window to get some more fresh air circulating. In these ways we can regulate our state of mind with postural and environmental changes. However if we're very sleepy, it may be best to put the meditation session on hold and have a lie down or put our feet up, perhaps even taking a short cat-nap if we're able to. In this way we can let our mind 'crash out' before we start to meditate and then come back to meditate with a fresh mind a little later.

There's the question of whether meditation is a luxury or a necessity. Saying that everyone needs to meditate might sound somewhat evangelical. We need to think about this though because apart from meditation when else do we get an opportunity to rest our minds? When we put our feet up at the end of the day or lie down to go to sleep, we might think we're having a rest, but generally we're just resting our bodies – our minds are still busy thinking about things as we drift off to sleep. It's only when we meditate that we actually rest our minds. Meditation is mainly about controlling our mind and involves developing our mind in a very specific way. Developing our mindfulness in particular is what gives us the ability to control our mind. Imagine a world in which everyone was meditating everyday. Probably most of the problems in the world would be resolved quite quickly. Is meditation necessary? Is controlling carbon production necessary? From one point of view it might not be necessary, but the world's going to fall apart eventually if we don't.

The explanations above give us some idea of how we can progress in meditation and in particular what sort of things we should be looking out for at the beginning of our practice. Acceptance, being more aware of what's going on in our mind, and becoming more adept at bringing our mind back without getting involved in a struggle - these are the key monitoring tools to begin with. There's a lot of work to do in these areas, and a lot of benefit to be gained from these alone. For as long as we're trying to apply these techniques, we'll be making progress. I've also given you an idea of how meditation develops beyond the initial stages, so that you have a greater sense of direction from the beginning.

Chapter 6:
Motivation

The focus for this chapter is motivation, which is an important aspect of meditation practice. On the audio MP3 there a couple of minutes near the beginning where I guide you through some motivational meditation. The idea here is to generate a special motivation for the meditation session that we're doing, so that we have more energy to apply in our session. Doing this gives us more strength to bring back our mind when it wanders, because we've made that extra effort to motivate ourselves at the beginning. Motivation in meditation is important in many ways because it's easy to lose sight of it. Meditation is the kind of thing that if we do it over and over again, we can end up doing it by rote, just going through the motions. Perhaps we feel like we should be doing it or we've established a time of day when we do it, and it becomes almost an unconscious activity, part of our routine, like brushing our teeth – but we've forgotten why we're doing it anymore.

It's important to stay in touch with our motivation and keep it alive. One helpful way to do this is to connect with our original intention. Just close your eyes for a minute and try to recall your original intention for wanting to learn about meditation. Go back to the original impulse that led you to want to meditate, including the reasons and circumstances surrounding that, why you were feeling this might be beneficial for you. Think about this for a little while and in this way try to bring that original motivation into the fore of your consciousness. Take a minute or two now to try this...

In recalling our original intention, we generate a pure and powerful motivation in our mind. If we ever feel that our motivation is lagging a little or getting mixed up with everything else that's going on in our life, it's helpful to take some time to go back to that original impulse, as we've just done now. Our original intention at some level is keeping us going with our meditation practice, whether we're aware of it or not. It's there in the background somewhere and it's helpful for us to be conscious of it.

Going back to 'square one' like this from time to time is a valuable tool to keep us on track and keep our meditation practice feeling fresh and alive. In the Zen tradition they talk of 'beginner's mind', which in the context of meditation practice entails approaching every meditation session like a beginner, as if it's the first time we've ever done it, and this brings great energy, enthusiasm and openness to the whole process. If we can approach our sessions with this kind of attitude, we'll feel more fulfilled and our sessions will be more rewarding for us.

Our motivation will develop as our experience of meditation develops. We might read or hear about the benefits of meditation in great depth, but unless we have an understanding of these in our own experience, knowing these benefits intellectually will not have much power to influence our motivation. If we see an advertisement for a new product in the supermarket that we've never tasted before, we might be persuaded to try it, but we won't really know whether it's any good until we've actually tasted it ourselves, however much the manufacturers rave about it or however much we trust them. It's the same with meditation. We're going to develop our own experience in time which is going to inform and enhance our motivation.

Gradually we learn through our own experience how meditation helps us to feel more balanced, more calm, less agitated, less stressed, less worried, and so on. This is going to power our motivation further, and fuel us on to meditate more. Really there's almost no limit to how much we can expand our motivation. The more we meditate and the deeper we go, the more motivated we're going to become. Over time our motivation will naturally extend to others as well, because as we become more experienced in meditation other people around us will start to benefit as well. People will start to notice that there's some positive change in us, perhaps that we're calmer, more relaxed, or less uptight for example. This in turn is going to have a beneficial influence on our relationships with other people, both at home and at work. It's going to start to rub off on everyone that comes into contact with us, even strangers on the street. So directly or indirectly our meditation will have an influence on others as well. People might start to comment and notice that something's changed in us, that we seem to be more positive since we started meditating. In my experience this happens quite often for people and can be a powerful motivator. When other people indicate that something's happening, it can help us to realise that our meditation practice is really working.

Whether we like it or not, our meditation practice is actually improving the world. This might sound like a grandiose statement, but if we think about it carefully we'll appreciate that it's true. It might seem that we're only making a small difference, but if we reflect on the fact that we're all connected to each other in some way or another it's easier to appreciate the global impact. We may be familiar with the 'six degrees of separation' theory, whereby everyone on the planet is connected to everyone else by no more than six personal connections. On this basis then, any benefit that we're giving to another person is going to affect positively the people that they're connected to, and so there's a domino effect that happens because we're all connected like this. We're not independent islands as we seem to think we are. Embracing this bigger picture is helpful in making our motivation stronger.

A lot of people these days are interested in making a positive change in the world. At some level we're doing that by making a positive change within our own mind, because this alone is going to have a universal effect. So we can make our motivation as big as we like. Again, whether we like it or not, our meditation practice is going to benefit the whole world. We can embrace this if we like, which will add great power to our meditation practice.

There are also some common pitfalls relating to motivation in meditation. One of the main pitfalls is discouragement. When we get discouraged in our meditation practice it is generally because we're not meeting our expectations. This is usually an indication that our expectations are unrealistic, a common problem when starting out in meditation. Our expectations of meditation are often too high. We set the bar too high and when we don't reach it, we feel discouraged, lose interest and eventually give up. We feel that things should be moving faster than they are, or that we should be progressing more rapidly, seeing more changes. Generally speaking, meditation is a slow process. There are some people that progress quickly but in my experience they're generally quite rare – for the majority of people meditation is a slow and gradual process, and not a 'quick fix' phenomenon.

Meditation addresses mental patterns that are very deeply ingrained. I often use the analogy of erosion to help to explain the way that meditation works. If we think about rocks or cliffs on the sea-front for example, the waves crash against the rocks over and over again time, and over a long period of time there's a visible change such that we can see that the rocks have eroded. However if we sit on the beach every day and watch, we're probably not going to see much change. Every time a wave hits, there is at least some subtle change taking place, at a cellular level say, but it's so microscopic that we're generally not going to see anything happening. If we had no knowledge of erosion and someone told us, 'The waves actually make the rocks get smaller,' and we sat down and watched to observe this, we'd probably give up and go home very quickly.

It's the same with meditation. It's a slow process, but subtle changes are taking place every time we do it. For example there have been numerous research studies conducted in recent years on the neurological and physiological effects of meditation, showing electro-magnetic changes taking place in the brain, reduced heart rate, and reduced blood pressure. In terms of how we actually feel inside, we might not notice any big changes straight away, but if we stick with it then gradually over time more noticeable changes will take place. Meditation is something that everyone can do, and as long as we don't have high expectations, as long as we keep trying, we can be sure that we are making progress, even if it's not immediately visible. What really matters is that we just try our best every time we meditate. It doesn't matter how much progress we appear to make in each session and what results we achieve. It's better to give up on the idea of results and just concentrate on trying our best. If we do this, the results will come naturally, on their own accord. The cliffs on the seafront will eventually crumble and recede, because the waves keep coming, and it's the same with meditation.

Meditation is an empowering way to improve our health and well-being. With meditation we have the tools and the power to do something about our situation. Difficult situations can even strengthen our meditation practice. In general our motivation in meditation can vary in relation to the extent of our problems. For example if we have sought out meditation due to experiencing great difficulties in our life, we may in fact be more motivated, because of those difficulties, to apply ourselves to the practice. If we have just an intellectual interest or curiosity, we may not have much drive to practice and progress in meditation.

It's also easy to become complacent with our meditation practice, for example we might start thinking 'I'm feeling much better now, I don't really need to meditate any more.' If this happens and we stop meditating, we'll eventually find that when difficulties start to arise in our life again, we're back where we started, struggling to cope internally. Sometimes difficult circumstances can be helpful in motivating us to go a bit further in our meditation practice, ultimately taking us to a better place in our mind.

Meditation is more a process of undoing something than constructing something. Primarily we are learning to let go of unwanted thoughts, as opposed to creating a desired internal state. It's ultimately about getting in touch with the true nature of our mind, the clarity and stillness that is within us, rather than constructing a fabricated mental state, which is like a house built on rocky ground. The more we meditate, the more we will understand this, as we tap in to the power of our own mind.

The other area that we can struggle with in terms of motivation is procrastination. We want to meditate at some level, but just never seem to get round to it. It's always later or tomorrow. One thing that can help with this is scheduling a regular time for our meditation and generally trying to be more disciplined about it. This isn't essential, and may be difficult depending on our personal schedule, but it's important to prioritise our meditation practice in our mind. Where does meditation sit on our list of priorities today for instance? Suppose we've got all the things that we need to do, or want to do, on a given day written down on a list, in order of priority. Where does our meditation practice go on that list? There's a Tibetan saying that daily chores are like an old man's beard - they grow back as soon as you shave them off. So for example as soon as we've finished the washing up, there's something else to clean, or something else to cook, or something else to do in the house, or someone else to entertain or talk to, or whatever it is. There's an incessant stream of things to do. There isn't actually a moment when we get to the end of our list. There's always something else to do and meditation often ends up at the bottom of the list or just keeps being shoved further and further down it. From one point of view we're never going to get all our jobs done. We will probably die with a list of things to do.

So it's important to make our meditation practice a priority every day. We can't avoid doing all the daily chores, and in the next chapter we'll look at integrating meditation with all those activities. But in a way our meditation session is most important in that it's nourishing the most important part of us - our internal state and wellbeing - and if that's not right, then nothing else is going to be right. The quality of our daily experience depends on the quality of our internal state. If our internal state is unsettled, then everything else is going to be unsettled in our day.

So if we can make the time, and it is really is about making the time, to do our meditation session regularly, we will transform our daily experience. If we can't manage to do it every day, that's okay - this is discussed in the next chapter. The key thing is to make it a regular part of our life and keep it near the top of our list of priorities, if not at the top of our list. The other stuff can wait - we'll get it done eventually, or perhaps we'll never get it done, but we'll probably stay on top of it for the most part. Fifteen minutes of meditation every day isn't going to throw our life into chaos. Quite the opposite in fact. Reflecting in this way can help us to avoid procrastination.

The last thing I want to address in relation to motivation is that sometimes our motivation can become unhealthy. So far I've discussed how we can lose our motivation, but how might our motivation become unhealthy? In some cases people's motivation for meditation can become self-centred, where they are using their meditation practice to run away or escape from other people or situations – an extension of the 'bury your head in the sand' syndrome. Meditation is ultimately about becoming more open and more warmly disposed towards other people, because as we become more experienced in meditation, we start to dissolve the habitual self-consciousness that inhibits our relations with others and creates barriers between us. Through meditation we start to melt and dissolve our self-consciousness over time, which I address in more depth in the final chapter.

Most of our negativity towards other people arises because our mind is unsettled and disturbed in some way. When our mind is calm, it's naturally warmly disposed towards other people. So if through our meditation practice we notice that we are starting to feel more warmly disposed towards others, then this is a sign that we are practising correctly. If on the other hand we find that we are becoming more selfish in some way, then we need to check our motivation to see if we're becoming self-centred in our approach to meditation. It can be difficult to notice this because our ego can easily play tricks with our mind. It can creep in to anything positive that we're doing in our life. Meditation can sometimes upset our ego as well – it pushes it out of the way which can force the ego to flare up and kick back. This can happen at any stage in our practice, even if we've been meditating for years.

So it's possible that our motivation can become distorted, perhaps egotistical or self-centred in some way, and this I would describe as an 'unhealthy' motivation. If this happens, it can be very helpful to go back to our original intention, which I discussed earlier. Generally this motivation is quite pure in its quality, normally arising in response to some difficulty in our life or some problems that we've had. This is where we want to be coming from when we're approaching our meditation practice.

Sometimes people can become quite 'puffed up' about their meditation practice, a bit full of themselves. It can become a status thing - 'I can meditate for hours' or 'I'm an advanced meditator' - a kind of spiritual pride, which is essentially just another manifestation of ego. This isn't so common, but it can happen, and again blocks us from making progress in our meditation practice.

Therefore it's important to keep an eye on our motivation and ideally to keep it fresh, healthy and alive. If every time we meditate we generate a positive, 'healthy' motivation and then apply this to our session, there will be little chance for our ego to creep in and interfere. We can think about the genuine benefits of meditation and determine, 'I'm going to make the most of this fifteen minutes, and am really going to try my best.' When we pause to reflect on our motivation in this way, we are engaging in a more contemplative form of meditation. We're thinking about the reasons why we're doing it and about the benefits of what we're doing. This is a reflective exercise, a contemplative process, which forms part of our fifteen-minute meditation. In this case it's a preparation for our actual training – the practice of developing our mindfulness by focusing on our breath.

Motivational meditation (to include at the beginning of the meditation session):

Bring to mind your original intention, the pure impulse that led you to take an interest in meditation, recalling the context of that intention. Just bring this to the fore of your mind. Then also bring to mind any experience that you have gained of the benefits of meditation for yourself. And also reflect on how your meditation practice is indirectly having a beneficial influence on others around you. And with this motivation in your mind, apply this now to your meditation session, thinking 'For all these reasons, I'm going to make the most of this session now. I'm going to try my best.'

Chapter 7:
Making it Part of Your Life

This chapter is about making meditation part of our life, which involves both establishing a regular meditation practice and also integrating our experience of meditation into our daily activities, applying it to whatever we're doing and whatever situations arise. Firstly we need to think about how to set up our meditation practice effectively. The concept of meditating every day is something that is encouraged in the sense that it then becomes part of our daily routine, making it easier for us to stay on top of it. If we start off doing it less frequently than this, it's at least helpful to have some kind of structure in order to maintain some regularity with our practice. The danger is that if we follow a freestyle approach at the beginning, our practice will quickly fall apart. Having some kind of structure is helpful at least to start with, to build a good foundation of experience. If it's not going to be every day, for whatever reason, then we can try doing it two or three times a week. However it's best to fit it in with our daily routine if we can.

This can be challenging, as there's a lot going on in our lives. However fifteen minutes is not a huge amount of time to squeeze in to our day, and if we can fit it in, we'll definitely feel better for it. Take a minute now to look at your daily routine as it stands, and list all the things that you do every day. For example, we might brush our teeth every day and have a shower every day and so on. Why do we do all these things? What is it about these daily rituals that we perform?

For example, why do we brush our teeth every day? We might say, 'Well, it's because the dentist told me to,' or 'That's because I know that if I don't, my teeth are going to decay'. And why do we have a shower or bath every day? We want our body to be clean and presentable in the world.

So why don't we spend some time cultivating and maintaining a good mental state every day, really developing our mental calm and settling our mind? If we don't do that, then our mind just goes all over the place. That's what happens if we don't give our mind regular attention - it starts to fall apart and get out of control. Then other problems begin to manifest, such as mental symptoms of ill health. Most people don't think of themselves as having mental health issues, but I would generally say that everyone has mental health issues to some extent. It may not warrant a psychiatric referral, but everyone has some disharmony in their mental state. We like to pretend that we don't, that we're 'fine'. A lot of us are in denial about the real state of our mind. We accept a level of unhappiness and mental unrest that we don't think we can do anything about, and don't really feel responsible for either. At what point do we take responsibility for our own mental state? Practising meditation is about taking that responsibility, just as we take responsibility for looking after our body. Most of us do things every day to look after our body. Why don't we give that same amount of attention to looking after our mind?

With meditation we have the tools to do this. Ideally we need to make meditation part of our daily routine. In some Eastern cultures meditation is something that most people do every day as a matter of course. It's something they don't even think twice about, they just do it, every day. Sadly meditation isn't deemed so important in Western culture, although it is gradually becoming more popular. It's a question of building it into our routine, so that we don't think of it as an 'extra' activity anymore, or as a treat or luxury even. We just think of it as part of looking after ourselves, part of the daily routine of taking care of ourselves. And as explained previously, it's not just for our own sake either – it's for the benefit of everyone around us as well.

If we can't manage to fit it in to our daily routine for whatever reason – and there are some of us who find this difficult – then we should try to create some sort of structure, whether it's on Tuesdays, Thursdays and Saturdays, for example, or just on the weekends. We might ask, 'Does it still work if I don't do it every day?'. It's better than doing nothing at all – there is still some benefit, for sure, even if we just do it every Sunday morning for example. There is a trade-off here in that if we're not doing it so regularly, we might lose track of our progress, but we can at least take the edge off things and maintain some level of internal calm. Some of us have such busy lives that it's very difficult to fit it in, but it's better to work it in somehow than not at all.

We should at least try to maintain the aspiration to do it, because some space might open up in our life at some point or our life circumstances might change, and then suddenly we've got more time to do it. If we can keep our meditation practice going in some shape or form, even if it's just on the back burner, then the aspiration to practice will stay with us and it can all open up for us in the future if circumstances allow. Ultimately though it's really about us making the time for it, not about finding time where there appears to be no time. It's more about making a space for it in our life, and, as mentioned earlier, taking responsibility.

Sometimes when we get sick, we might feel that we can't meditate temporarily. It's hard to meditate sometimes when we are unwell because we don't have the energy. Actually though we can meditate when we're sick, even if we're lying in bed. Generally when we are unwell, there is an imbalance in our body as well as in our mind. We can sense that things are a bit shaky and unsettled, both physiologically and mentally. Settling our mind in this instance can catalyse the healing process on both a mental and physical level. It is generally more difficult to work with our mind in meditation when we're unwell, but it is worth trying if we can.

Many people ask, 'What time of day is best for meditation?'. The time that we meditate each day will of course depend on our schedule, and to some extent also what works for us best. Generally it's better to meditate in the morning because our mind's fresher then, and also it sets us up well for the day ahead. It's like getting out of bed on the right foot. However it really depends on us and what works for us best. There's no rule here really. Some people find it easier to meditate in the early evening, some just before bed, and some in the morning. It can vary from person to person. If we like we can set ourselves a regular time each day, like 7.30am or 6.30pm for example. In some cases it's good to have a backup time as well, if for whatever reason we miss our regular time-slot. It can be helpful to have in our mind a second option like this. It's also best not to meditate straight after eating a meal, as the digestive process can make us sleepy.

It's also useful to have a dedicated space for our meditation practice. This doesn't mean we need to have a separate room in our house for it, but if there's a certain chair that we like to use for meditation, or a certain place where we like to sit, that can be quite helpful. Sitting in the same place every time we meditate makes it easier for our mind, in that it limits our distractions. Our familiarity with that place means that there's nothing new of interest to our mind there anymore. We get used to being in that space, such that we're no longer interested in the sounds and noises and visual appearances and whatever else is going on there. We become accustomed to it, whether it's sitting in a special chair or a corner of a room or a cushion on the floor or a place on our bed. That's not to say that we must always meditate there – our meditation practice can be flexible, but it's beneficial to have a special place for it, at least when we're starting out. The Tibetans call their meditation seat their 'happy seat', an encouraging way of thinking about it. If we want to go a bit further, we can add some calming elements to our space, such as a candle for example. The idea is to create a special zone for our meditation.

However, as just mentioned, meditation is ultimately very flexible and not something that we necessarily have to do in a formal setting. It's something that we can do anywhere and at any time. As explained earlier, when we're ill, we can be lying down in our bed meditating. We can do it while travelling, on the bus, train, or aeroplane for example - although preferably not while we're driving a car! There are many ways to meditate, in a variety of different contexts. So don't feel limited to your special meditation space at home. There are so many opportunities to meditate every day. For example we might find that we've got five minutes at work where we have a quiet moment to ourselves, and we can just go inside and do a little meditation right there. It doesn't have to be the full fifteen minutes, even just a couple of minutes can be beneficial. At any point in the day when we feel like our mind is getting a little out of control, we can just come back in and gather ourselves with a few moments of focusing on the breath, for example. It can make a real difference. Another concept is training in mindfulness with our eyes open, for example when we're walking down the street or exercising. In these situations we can also be focusing on our breath, trying to keep our mind calm and letting go of distractions.

I've explained previously three qualities that we're developing in meditation. One of these is contentment, which is that feeling of being at peace and being fully satisfied in the present moment, for example when we are calmly holding our attention on the breath. If we can experience this contentment in meditation, we can experience it in other areas of our life as well. Whenever we find our mind wanting more, desiring things, or feeling discontent, we can just stop for a moment and try to settle our mind to find that contentment again. The irony of our desire or craving is that the things that we crave don't actually satisfy us. They give us a few fleeting moments of pleasure and then we're without it again. There's no genuine contentment there. If we can establish real contentment from within our own mind through meditation, then we'll find that we are less wanting, less unsettled and less agitated in our daily life. With any feeling of dissatisfaction there is agitation in the mind.

Another problem is that we are not accepting of what's happening in our mind. Unwanted thoughts come up and we push them away. There's judgement and non-acceptance in our mind, not just in meditation but all the time, and not just with respect to our thoughts. We also push things away and push people away. Someone comes along and we don't like the look of them - our first reaction is to push them away, not necessarily physically but mentally. We're either pushing away things that we don't like or pulling things in that we do like – constantly pushing and pulling. The mind of acceptance helps us to change this, so that we are more at peace with whatever is happening around us. We're not fighting it or pushing it away. We're accepting of whatever comes up. We then have the space to change things, if we need to. Acceptance doesn't mean being passive. It gives us the mental clarity and calm to act appropriately and in the best way.

The third quality that I explained earlier is developing our awareness and being present, which is something we can be doing in every aspect of our life, whether at work or spending time with our family or friends. It's about being present with whatever or whoever we're focusing on, being conscious and aware, in an undistracted way. Even contemplating and reflecting on things in an undistracted way is a form of meditation.

There's such a force of distraction in our society these days. We can go into a shopping mall for example and the atmosphere there is so frenzied, pervaded by dissatisfaction. Even people that have bought something are only satisfied for a short while, and then it's over, and then 'What's next?'. Advertisements are constantly telling us about the next best thing that we need to buy. It's never-ending. If we simplify our lives, we are ultimately forced to look within. Initially this can be painful as we experience withdrawal from the things that we've grown dependent on. However we will soon appreciate the deeper fulfilment that comes from a peaceful and contented mind.

Occasionally it can be helpful to set aside a morning or a day where we focus on our meditation practice a bit more than usual. This would generally be referred to as a 'retreat', in that for a set period of time we are retreating from our normal daily activities and emphasising our meditation practice. A retreat like this gives us an opportunity to go deeper in our practice. Perhaps we're coasting at a certain level in our practice, but after a day's retreat we feel like we've moved up a level. It's like we reach a new plateau. The change may be small, but is often significant. In the longer term this can be an important part of progressing and going deeper in our practice.

Retreat is something we can do on our own or in a group setting. If you're doing it on your own, try starting with just a morning – you might want to try being silent for a period of time, and do two or three sessions of meditation during the morning, between which you take time to reflect or do peaceful things. If we're doing a whole day, then we might do four or five meditations in total. We can do longer retreats if we like, but it's best to start small and build up to those. I wouldn't recommend that you dive into a ten day retreat straight away, as you might easily get overwhelmed.

These are some suggestions for establishing and maintaining a daily meditation practice and integrating it into our daily life.

Chapter 8:
Going Deeper

This final chapter explains a deeper level of the meditation practice, addressing a more subtle obstruction. When we start doing this practice we generally have a sense of our breath that we're focusing on being 'over there' and our self being 'back here' somewhere. There's a sense of distance or separation between us and the sensation of the breath that we're meditating on. This can manifest as an interference in our practice and also lies at the root of the distractions in our mind.

If we start to develop a feeling of being bored with meditation, this generally stems from this sense of duality between our mind and the sensation of our breath. We have a sense of our self meditating that is isolated from our breath, and thus there's a feeling of something missing in our experience. We're not fully engaged in the experience, and this is why we can start feeling bored sometimes. This sense of an isolated self is actually the problem here. It's not that the meditation isn't working, but that we are feeling removed from it in some way.

How do we break through this duality so that we can be fully engaged in meditation? The first thing is to develop an awareness of that duality in our own experience, looking within our mind at this isolated sense of self that is present while we're focusing on the sensation of our breath. We need to observe this sense of separation that is holding us back from fully engaging with the breath. Try to see how there is this sense of self in your mind as well as the sensation of your breath - 'I am here, my breath is there.' We keep our main attention on the breath, but observe this duality from a corner of our mind.

Having observed this for a short time, we then try to allow our mind to merge completely with the sensation of our breath, letting go of this sense of self, so that all we experience is the sensation of our breath. It should feel as if our mind has merged completely with the subtle sensation of our breath. All that is happening in our mind at this point is the awareness of our breath, as if it were unowned, not belonging to anyone, just a mere sensation. We try to let go completely of the sense of our self meditating, and engage completely with the sensation of our breath until it pervades our whole awareness.

The experience of fully engaging with our meditation object in this way is very powerful and deeply healing. If we are able to let go of that sense of our self meditating and be fully engaged with the breath in our session, we will experience a deep feeling of letting go. Initially this experience can be a little daunting for some people, due to our clinging to this sense of self habitually and constantly. However if we stay with it we will gradually start to feel more comfortable.

What we're dealing with here is an isolated sense of self which is essentially a mistaken view of our self. It's not in tune with reality. We feel isolated and cut off from others at a deep level, such that we have an unhealthy preoccupation with our own welfare. The aim of this practice is to develop and improve our health and well-being. At the deepest level I would say that perfect health depends on letting go of this isolated sense of self in our mind, and developing a balanced sense of self that is more in tune with reality.

When we do the meditation in this deeper way, and immerse ourselves into our meditation object, in this case the breath, we effectively 'lose ourselves' temporarily. Don't worry, you'll still be there when the meditation's over! You're not going to disappear or vanish. This experience of letting go, even for a few moments, is very powerful and healing on a deep level, and ultimately this is the direction in which we want to go with our meditation practice. In the longer term this is a goal for us to work towards. Many people talk of 'losing themselves' in various experiences, such as listening to a piece of music, dancing, or being in nature, and generally this is similar to what I'm talking about here, in that there is that deep feeling of letting go, letting our guard down, and engaging ourselves fully in a particular experience.

Applying this deeper approach in our meditation also helps us to connect more deeply with others because we're loosening that barrier between ourselves and others. We're letting go of that construct in our mind that makes us feel separate and isolated from others.

Don't worry if at this stage you're unable to engage your mind fully in the way I'm describing here. We may not be able to let go of our sense of self in the meditation, but at least we can try to be aware of it, and this in itself can help to quieten our mind. It's a bit like a school teacher writing on the blackboard with her back turned to the class, while one of her students starts causing trouble in the classroom – when the teacher turns around and makes eye contact with the trouble-maker, there is normally a quietening effect. Similarly people report that when they are able to observe their sense of self in the meditation they find that their meditation session is generally quieter, with less distraction. This is a clear indication that our isolated sense of self lies at the root of the distractions in our mind.

Guided Meditation MP3

A 15-minute guided meditation MP3 with the same title accompanies this book, and is available separately from most online MP3 retailers, including the Amazon MP3 Store.

Search MP3 store by 'Sam May' or by MP3 title '15-Minute Meditation for Health and Wellbeing'.

Printed in Great Britain
by Amazon

16592146R00036